MW01288951

BUILD A MONEY MACHINE

PENG JOON

POWERED BY

B O O K S

BUILD A MONEY MACHINE

MAKE MONEY ONLINE,
ESCAPE THE 9-5, AND LIVE AN AWESOME LIFE

PENG JOON

Copyright © PENG JOON
2nd edition, MMXVI

ALL RIGHTS RESERVED. No part of this book may be reproduced or transmitted in any form whatsoever, electronic, or mechanical, including photocopying, recording, or by any informational storage or retrieval system without the expressed written, dated and signed permission from the author.

Author: PENG JOON
Title: BUILD A MONEY MACHINE
Category: SELF-HELP/General

Publisher:
Black Card Books
Division of Gerry Robert Enterprises Inc.
Suite 214 , 5-18 Ringwood Drive
Stouffville, Ontario
Canada, L4A 0N2
International Calling: 1 647 361 8577
www.blackcardbooks.com

LIMITS OF LIABILITY / DISCLAIMER OF WARRANTY: The author and publisher of this book have used their best efforts in preparing this material. The author and publisher make no representation or warranties with respect to the accuracy, applicability or completeness of the contents. They disclaim any warranties (expressed or implied), merchantability for any particular purpose. The author and publisher shall in no event be held liable for any loss or other damages, including but not limited to special, incidental, consequential, or other damages. The information presented in this publication is compiled from sourced believed to be accurate, however, the publisher assumes not responsibility for errors or omissions. The information in this publication is not intended to replace or substitute professional advice. The author and publisher specifically disclaim any liability, loss, or risk that is incurred as a consequence, directly or indirectly, of the use and application of any of the contents of this work.

THIS BOOK IS FOR:
YOU

BLUEPRINT

Prologue: Manifesto

Part I

1. Study Hard, Get A Good Job, Die

2. I Wish I Had Flunked Out Of University Because That Would Make A Better Story

3. Standing In The Shower And Getting Wet But Not Showering

Step 2: Milking The Content Cow

Fresh Unique Content. Setting up your business and establishing your brand without doing any of the hard work..

Step 3: Getting People Excited Over Something They Didn't Know They Wanted

Product Promotion. Getting the word out in more ways than one and achieving success by piggybacking on the shoulders of giants.

Step 4: Reeling In Ideal Customers

Get Targeted Traffic. Advice you should absolutely never follow and legit techniques that will bring in the cash flow.

Step 5: Make More Money By Working Less

Automate. Created and perfected, now duplicated many times over. Complete your personal money machine and gain financial freedom..

PROLOGUE: MANIFESTO

Your dreams fulfilled in three pages.

Imagine waking up in the morning. No boss. No alarm clock. You head to your workplace. A seven-second commute from your bed. You check your email and realize you made more money asleep than you did when you were awake. You answer a couple of emails telling other people what to do. It takes you about 18 minutes. And your workday is complete. You now have the entire day ahead of you, to do whatever you want.

If this sounds like a lifestyle you'd be interested in… then you're in the right place… because I'm going to show you how I made a ton of cash online and how you can do it too.

Now I could say something like 'this is the start of a brand new chapter in your life'… But to be honest, it really depends on whether you're actually going to do anything with the information I give you.

I'm not a miracle worker. I'm just a guy who figured out Internet marketing the hard way. And in this book I'm going to simplify, compile and present everything I know to you. So you can do what I did to generate my first million dollars online.

No, I wasn't born with a silver spoon in my mouth.

I worked for it. And earned it. If you think I'm arrogant for saying so, then you're going to be in for a shocker because the rest of these pages are a blueprint of how I achieved that success. Plus a bunch of awesome stories in between that will probably offend you.

I believe in transparency.

It's gotten me into trouble before, for reasons that I will continue to share with you throughout this book. I tend to call things the way I see them. Figuratively, my life is an open book. You only need to Google my name to read my story. It's all public domain. Well, the edited universal version anyway. And of course now, my life is literally in this open book. The only difference is that I'm giving away everything this time. It's the PG13 version. My voice on paper. And my proven five-step system to generate a passive online income laid out for you to use.

This is the actual system I use on a daily basis to make a lot of money online.

Because let's face it, the Internet is home to endless potential wealth. Enough to go round, twice over.

It's up to them, and you, to decide whether or not you want to tap into that cash stream and generate the income you deserve.

You see, it's during my seminar, *Internet Income Intensive,* that I walk my students through the ins and outs of successfully starting an online business. I've taught this program in over 20+ countries around the world and lucky for you, you're going to receive all that guidance right here. Because I'm awesome like that.

If you're not completely disgusted yet and still want to read on, then I'd like to welcome you to the start of a brand new chapter in your life.

Because you're reading this right now, I know that you want more in life.

You have bigger dreams than what you're currently living.

For some it's a burning desire to quit their jobs and be financially free forever. For others it might just be finding a way to supplement their income.

Whatever it is, this is the be all and end all of books that will revolutionize everything you thought you knew about the Internet. Damn right.

"To laugh often and much;

*To win the respect of intelligent people
and the affection of children;*

*To earn the appreciation of honest critics
and endure the betrayal of false friends;*

To appreciate beauty,

To find the best in others;

To leave the world a bit better,

Whether by a healthy child,

A garden patch,

Or a redeemed social condition;

*To know even one life has breathed easier
because you have lived.*

This is to have succeeded."

– RALPH WALDO EMERSON

- PART I -

HOW TO MAKE MONEY ONLINE

---

*Well that's what I'm going
to show you.*

*But first let me tell you how
it all started.*

- 1 -

STUDY HARD, GET A GOOD JOB, DIE

*Do not go where the path may lead,
go instead where there is no path
and leave a trail.*

That subtitle is a quote from Ralph Waldo Emerson. I tried to reword it so that you'd think I was profound. But that quote pretty much sums up my entire upbringing.

I grew up in a conservative Asian middle-class family.

My father, my role model, is the most hardworking man I know. He worked a full-time 9-5 job as a scientist for the government.

And, he won an award for discovering a new strain of papaya. On top of that he had a durian farm. Every day after work he would labor over that farm as well as throughout the weekend. In my opinion that added up to a full eight days a week of work.

Yes, I wrote eight. No, it's not a typo.

And even though he worked every possible hour available, it was a hard life for us. And I hated it.

Now don't get me wrong.

I had a super supportive family and was surrounded by love. But because we didn't have much, I wanted more.

And my parents totally encouraged my ambition. Because they had worked hard their entire lives.

When I was a kid I asked my mom which of her friends earned the most money. And she said her remisier friend did. From that point forward I wanted to be a remisier. For years that was my goal. Be a remisier and make a ton of cash.

Then some time later I asked my mom how her remisier friend was doing. And I guess it must have been during some crashing economy period or whatever, so my mom said he had lost all his money and his life sucked.

Well not in those words, but that's all I heard.

She went on to say that if I really wanted a good life and a stable income and a lot of money, I should be a doctor.

So of course, from that moment on I wanted to be a doctor.

You see, that was the belief system I grew up with. From the start I feel I was groomed to get a good job and be a good employee.

My father's upbringing was the same.

We believed that in order to make money, we had to work hard. And if that money wasn't a direct result of hard work, then it must have involved some form of manipulation, dishonesty or scammy shit. The harder you work, the more money you'd get.

And it's true to a certain extent. But with only so many hours in the day, how can you possibly work more to earn more?

That was what I struggled to find out.

Nevertheless I was a fantastic son.

And I followed my parents' words to the T.

My father told me from the very start that he couldn't afford to send me overseas to study. I'd have to attend a local university. If I wanted to go overseas, it would have to be up to me to make that happen. I would have to earn it myself. Because of that, I studied my butt off at school and was a straight A student. (Not really. I was a naturally smart kid. I did the bare minimum and would always be top of the class). Teachers told me to go into the science stream because that lands all the good jobs. So I did. And when I didn't know what to study at uni, I was told to go into economics because I was good at it. So I did.

At that point in time, I was "on track." I received a conditional scholarship from JPA to the sum of $51,000 to the University of Warwick in the UK. Everything was going according to plan.

I was told to play safe and do what everyone else was doing.

But for me, working hard didn't work out.

13

- 2 -

I WISH I HAD FLUNKED OUT OF UNIVERSITY BECAUSE THAT WOULD MAKE A BETTER STORY

But it's still an awesome story.

So if you're not already aware of this portion of my story then here it is in a nutshell:

In university I partied, drank a lot and was addicted to a certain video game. My housemates would be smoking weed and were high everyday.

I barely passed.

My results were so poor I had to pay back the full conditional government scholarship I had been awarded.

$51,000.

I got a crappy job that gave me crappy pay.

I Googled "How to make money online."

Fast forward to today and I'm a millionaire.

The end.

Maaaaan. Writing a book is hard.

Ok.

Deep breath.

I really like gambling.

It's in my blood.

I'm Chinese.

We like to gamble. If ever you are overcome with an uncontrollable desire to find a Chinese guy in any country that you are currently in, go to a casino.

In my first year at uni, I was this skinny little 17-year old Chinese kid who was curious to see what the inside of a casino looked like. Living in the UK, away from my parents, completely independent and liberated.

I got myself a fake ID to enter a place called Stanley's Casino.

I lost all my money. I'm talking actual tuition money.

18

And because of that, I was crazy broke and couldn't leave my house for my entire second year of university.

Now one of my housemates at the time was an epic pothead and the air in the house was so constantly thick with smoke I swear we had to hack through it with a battle axe every time we needed to take a piss in the toilet.

I logged in a total of 13 hours at uni for my second and third year combined.

I'd wake up at the most random hours, to the point where I would literally have no idea what month it was.

One of the games we used to play to pass the time involved piling into our Ford Escort and smoking up. The person that could stay in the car the longest would emerge the champion of nothing.

Naturally no one wanted to be the first to get out.

And the smoke was beyond intoxicating. You didn't even have to breathe let alone take a drag to get stoned. It infiltrated through your flesh and broke your brain open to a manic buzz.

It was during a contest of epic proportions that the driver of said car decided to up the stakes on account of nobody wanting to quit.

He started making handbrake turns around the empty car park we were in. It was winter. The roads were icy. We were high.

20

We spun out of control and smashed into a lamppost.

Introducing (drumroll please): *World Of Warcraft.*

After nearly dying, my instinct for survival brought me to the discovery of the video game that would rule my life for several years to come.

Warcraft was cheap entertainment that was highly addictive and didn't require me to do a damn thing. And it certainly never caused me to ram into any lampposts. I was hooked.

My new and not-so-improved lifestyle consisted of instant noodles and take-out. Empty pizza boxes and dirty plates were stacked in my bedroom, which I rarely left.

Once a week, Wilson (the only one of us who actually attended classes) would shout at me to bring down my plates and wash them.

And that's how I nearly flunked out of university.

You may be wondering how I even managed to pass. Well to be honest it's because I'm gifted. Yeah.

I suppose my school background of being an overachiever helped.

But really it's because I'm gifted.

21

- 3 -

STANDING IN THE SHOWER AND GETTING WET BUT NOT SHOWERING

The point of no return that you will go through, right before you kick your ass into action.

Have you ever had those moments when you're standing in the shower and your mind just drifts off somewhere else? You get into the deepest train of thought that you forget all about actually showering and just end up getting wet.

Well, I experienced a profound shower moment that caused me to turn things around.

After graduating with a 3rd class, and an average of 42%, I returned home to a sexy debt of $51,000. That's in USD. My conditional scholarship from the government obviously had to be paid back because I sucked at uni.

I was unemployed, broke and in debt.

Yet I still thought I was the shit and was confident that people would want to hire me. Prior to leaving for the UK I was already being headhunted. Huge multinational companies were basically waiting for me to graduate so I could work for them.

Well that all shot to hell when they saw my grades.

So after three months of interviews I finally settled for a job selling credit cards.

During my time with the company I managed to make a grand total of two sales. My mom. And my dad. (See, I told you they were really supportive.)

After hopping around odd jobs I finally acquired a 'stable' profession as a financial consultant. My monthly salary was RM1,200 ($400 USD) and I stayed there for two years.

I dreaded going to work every morning, sitting through hours of traffic back and forth, forever looking forward to the weekend, only to repeat the same process all over again on Monday.

And I thought that was all there was to life. If you don't do well in your studies, you end up paying the price. I felt forced into a corner and couldn't survive on my own. I had to find a way to supplement my income.

I decided to get back to my former hardworking ways and became the go-to guy in the company I was working for. I was always the first one in and the last one out. I was the top contributor. I became an asset.

After a year, my boss called me into his office and sat me down. He told me how awesome I was. He was going to do something he had never done before. He gave me a 20% increment. That increased my salary from RM1,200 to RM1,400.

I understood that it was a huge increment percentage-wise… but c'mon. It still sucked.

Working my ass off for RM1,400. WTF.

I contemplated suicide and stood at the edge of the Twin Towers looking down on KL and wondered how my life had come to this.

No, not really.

The real story is I was in the shower one morning, thinking about how I'd reached this point in life. One of those showers where you just stand there getting wet and drift off to another universe.

I regretted all the stupid shit I'd done in university. I figured that this was my punishment for not studying, and that there would be no end to my crappy life.

From being the star student and getting a scholarship to studying abroad to ending up in a Chinaman company with shit pay. (Side note: My editor advised against using terms like Chinaman but

I believe since I'm Chinese I get to use it? It's like using the N word when you're… never mind.)

My parents were disappointed. And that was more humiliating and painful than having them be angry.

I was a disappointment.

Chinese New Year was my most hated time of the year because all the aunties (you know the ones I'm talking about) would gather and tut tut their perfectly permed heads at how bright my future had been and how I had thrown it all away.

And so I entered the term 'How to make money online' into Google.

Two billion search results were generated.

Fan-fucking-tastic.

But I jumped right in. I bought a crapload of eBooks and home-learning courses. Tried anything and everything. Back then I had no one to learn from and I did it all on my own through trial and error.

27

I was determined to turn things around for myself.

I'd spend 9-5 at my day job then stay back from 6 pm to 2 am working on my website. The Internet connection at the office was really fast and the printer was good. One time my boss sent me to Penang to settle some business thing. I did nothing but work on my site for the entire week.

After doing this for some time, my boss called me into his office and said, "Peng Joon, I've noticed you've been working even harder than ever now. Keep it up!"

Trolololol.

And finally after nine months of this, I got an email that changed my life.

DEFINITION: INFORMATION PRODUCT

An intangible good that provides information, knowledge or wisdom that the purchaser is seeking. Examples include eBooks, webinars, membership sites, video courses, downloadable guides, audiobooks etc.

Endless possibilities that the Internet offers, that nobody will ever tell you about.

- 4 -

MAKING A TON OF MONEY SELLING INFORMATION THAT PEOPLE COULD GET FOR FREE IF THEY WANTED TO

Endless possibilities that the Internet offers, that nobody will ever tell you about.

2**011**: Amazon's sales of digital books surpass the sales of paperback and hardcover books.

Digital products are the future.

2012: $185 billion worth of goods were sold online.

Yet many people still doubt that there is money to be made in digital information products.

2016: Tried to Google for proof that the market is even bigger today but the the first page didn't reveal hard numbers.

But yeah... it's bigger today okay? Just take my word for it.

Let's face it, starting a franchise or a brick and mortar business is expensive. The Internet business is the only business that is BOOMING.

32

And here's the funny thing I realized when I went into this whole Internet thing: The more obsessed about money you are, the more it will shy away from you.

I want you to think of making money as a result of serving and helping people. That's the key goal here. Because if you're in this with only your needs and desires as your sole purpose, then it's going to be difficult for you to generate an income.

Of course we all want to make money. And if you already have money, then it's only natural to want to make more money. It's human nature. Survival of the fittest. And there's nothing wrong with that.

But if you're prepared to sideline others, step over people and completely disregard the heart of this industry, then you're in for trouble.

Because what goes around comes around.

People often view making money online as something scammy and untrustworthy. For my parents, if you weren't putting blood, sweat and tears into your job, then it must have been immoral.

So here's the thing.

Information products give people information that they want.

As an Internet marketer, it is your duty to recommend great products that will genuinely provide solutions to real problems that people have. We are here to serve others. And the customer always comes first.

With my system, it would be easy for me to sell any old thing online that had zero value for $100. If people complained about it and asked for a refund, well I could make them run around in circles until they gave up and keep the money for myself.

But I won't.

And I never will.

My goal is to generate a fully-automated passive income through the Internet by helping other people live life on their terms. In my opinion, it's the only way to live.

I want you to readjust the way you approach and think about making money. Understand that money is a by-product and helping people is the goal. Cool?

One of the biggest reasons why people are afraid to even get started online is because they are not tech savvy.

I am not a programmer, nor am I a graphic designer or writer. These aspects don't matter.

What matters is the marketing. The good news is marketing is a learnable, training skill. And I'm going to be transferring that skill over to you. Because that's the skill that pays the bills.

Before we get down to it, I want to mention this first because it serves at the foundation. When it comes to getting better at anything in life, whether it's playing tennis, learning a new language, a musical instrument or in this case building an online business, I believe there are 3 ways to do anything. And these 3 different approaches will yield very different results in life.

35

1. Trying to do something

Most people operate at this level. I dare say this. Most people are starters. Dabblers. They're constantly starting and trying new things. When they reach an obstacle, challenge or plateau, they quit and try something else.

2. Doing your best

We're taught from young to "do your best." I know my mum used to tell me that all the time. Here's the problem. How do we know if we're doing our best based on our willingness or doing our best based on our capability? Because to "do your best" can be a very convenient excuse to not achieve something.

It's how people give themselves an out. They believe that whatever happens, it's ok, as long as they did their best.

If you've been living in a "do your best" mindset, I say fuck that shit. You need a new mentality. A mentality that breathes success. And that is:

3. "Whatever it takes"

36

And I don't mean rob a bank. Whatever it takes... as long as it's legal, moral and ethical. To understand that the path will be filled with struggles, challenges and obstacles. Honor that struggle. Because those are the days ordinary people will quit. And those are the days that will separate champions from ordinary people.

At any time if you're not getting the results you would like to have in whatever area of your life, ask yourself very honestly. Am I trying, am I doing my best or am I doing whatever it takes? All 3 approaches will yield very different results. Choose wisely.

Now I know some of you might think that was ra-ra mindset fluff, but that's played a huge part of my life and it's been a game changer for me. If that portion was too heavy, it's basically this: Don't do your best, do whatever it takes.

With that out of the way, let's talk about how it all started...

37

- 5 -

THE $7 THAT CHANGED MY LIFE FOREVER

Why a few bucks is all it takes to turn a fantasy into reality.

Well, after spending thousands of dollars on eBooks about how to make money online I figured out the one common denominator: Market an information product based on something you love.

Remember that epic addiction I had to World of Warcraft?

I had spent over 2,300 hours playing Warcraft back in uni. It was the main contributing factor to my very unproductive college years. In fact, I honestly believe it's the reason why I nearly flunked out, which lead to me not being able to secure a good job, and ultimately be in the crappy situation I found myself.

But that game was love. That was my passion.

So I wrote a 32-page guide on how to excel at the game and slapped on a $7 price tag.

With naïve enthusiasm I put up my first sales page and waited for the sales to roll in.

Nothing happened.

For nine full months.

Then early one morning as I was preparing to get ready for another monotonous day of work at a job I hated, I checked my email. It was 6:30 am. And there it was. One unread message. The subject was: Notification of Payment Received.

It was from PayPal. For $7. My jaw dropped. I couldn't believe it. My body was trembling with excitement and I wanted to shout and fist-pump all over the damn room. Just to be sure I looked at it again. And again. And again.

This was my first sale. I had never seen a message like that before.

I logged into my PayPal account and sure enough there it was. Like a shiny beacon of hope.

$7.

Just sitting there in my account. Money I had earned when a complete stranger from halfway across the world had decided to click the "Add To Cart" button and purchase my World of Warcraft guide online. It happened at exactly 4:12 am in local time. Meaning I got paid while I was asleep.

Getting paid to sleep.

Yes, I had to say it twice. Because this was one of the single most important life-changing turning points in my life.

I screamed for my mummy. Honestly I did. I was bouncing off the walls by that point and when my mum walked into my room I showed her my computer screen and told her I made a sale.

41

"You worked for nine months to make $7. Good job," was along the lines of her response. But I was so fired up by then nothing could bring me down.

There was a shift. I felt it. Physically, mentally, emotionally and (in a small $7 way) financially! My situation had changed. And I had changed along with it.

Because I realized that if I could do this once. I could do it again. It was at that point that I realized this shit is real. I had monetized my passion. The passion that had caused me to be in the crap situation I was in was now the saving grace that would propel me out of it.

How poetic.

And all I had to do was repeat the process. Which I did.

Ka-Ching.

DEFINITION: DIGITAL MARKETING

A term that refers to various and different promotional techniques deployed to reach customers, mainly using the Internet as a core medium. It embodies an extensive selection of service, product and brand marketing tactics. Considered more targeted, measurable and interactive.

Seriously. I have no idea what I just read. Yeah, I totally copy-pasted that shit off the Internet. What a load of mumbo jumbo. Those are the kind of sentences that turn my stomach.

DISCLAIMER:

43

Unlike many 'trainers' out there, I will not be teaching you theory. I did not read a marketing textbook to regurgitate that crap to you. I will only teach you stuff I personally do in my business.

ABRIDGED DEFINITION: DIGITAL MARKETING

Selling stuff online. Via the Internet.

What you don't know, why you're missing out and how to get onboard now.
VACANCY
* insert your name here *

- 6 -

THE BEST JOB IN THE WORLD HAS A VACANCY WITH YOUR NAME ON IT

What you don't know,
why you're missing out and
how to get onboard now.

The digital business is like a buffet. People come, pay, and serve themselves. And you never have to be there to greet them or collect the money hand-to-hand.

For us, people come to our websites, purchase the product and click a download button.

While you can have a very lucrative online business selling tangible items like clothes and gadgets, the great thing about getting into the digital marketplace is you don't have to deal with stuff like cost, overheads, inventory, warehousing and shipping. You're selling information. And this information is already prepared, written and can be sold multiple times over. It never runs out.

Plus, as I mentioned before, it can be automated. That first sale I made happened at 4 am while I was asleep. I didn't have to entertain a customer or punch buttons in a cash register or give back exact change. Because I already had a system in place (which I'll be going through step-by-step next), that customer came to me, liked what I had to offer and made his purchase.

If you're thinking that this may be something you're interested in being a part of, good. Because anybody can do it. Anybody.

You don't need to be an expert. You don't need to be techy. I'm neither and I still made it work. The only think that you need to focus on is the marketing. Which is exactly what I'll be showing you how to do.

And the most powerful part of all this is your worldwide market. As long as someone has access to the Internet, they can potentially buy your product. So think on a bigger scale. I target the U.S. because of their high purchasing power. What that means is I earn in US dollars. And that's yummy.

47

- 7 -

ARE THERE ANY MONKEYS IN YOUR LIFE?

Ooh-ooh, ahh-ahh.

Stephenson, G. R. (1967). Cultural acquisition of a specific learned response among rhesus monkeys.

[This is the actual name of the study. And I formatted it legit bibliography style. Originally I wanted to rename it. These are the titles I came up with: Cultural study on monkeys, Monkeys are the shit, The cultural education of monkeys, A study I found online that is awesomeballs, and A scientific study that ties in with a cute question I want to ask you at the end. So let's get to it.]

THE EXPERIMENT - PART I

Five monkeys are locked in a cage. A banana is hung from the ceiling with a ladder placed beneath it.

Naturally a monkey would run up the ladder to grab the banana. But as soon as the monkey starts to climb, the researcher would spray ice cold water on him and the four other monkeys in the cage.

When another monkey attempted to climb the ladder, the researcher would again spray all the monkeys with ice cold water.

This was repeated until they learned their lesson:

Climbing the ladder means ice cold water for everyone. Therefore no one climbed the ladder.

THE EXPERIMENT - PART II

When the five monkeys were trained to not climb the ladder, the researcher replaced one of the first-generation monkeys with an inexperienced one.

The new monkey saw the banana and immediately made his way to the ladder. But the other four monkeys pulled him back and beat him up.

So the new guy learns this lesson:

Climbing the ladder means getting beaten up. Therefore don't climb the ladder. He doesn't even get sprayed with water.

The process is repeated three more times with a new monkey added at every cycle. It was discovered that every new monkey, who had never received the cold water treatment, would join the others and beat up the new guy that tried to climb the ladder.

THE EXPERIMENT - PART III

All the first-generation monkeys have been replaced with second-generation monkeys.

51

A new third-generation monkey is placed in the cage. It runs to the ladder to get the banana but is stopped and beaten up by the others.

None of the second generation monkeys have *ever* been sprayed with water. They have *no explanation* as to their actions.

But they have been hardwired to do things that way. And so it remains.

CONCLUSION:

Sometimes we do things because we are told to by others without reason, who were told to by others without reason, who were told to by others without reason...

And that original reason is not only lost, but very likely is no longer valid to the current situation.

When I started my journey with digital marketing and trying to make money online, I had a lot of people trying to stop me. To talk me out of it. Telling me it was a bad idea, a waste of time, a silly investment.

And the most vocal of those people were the ones closest to me, who genuinely cared and loved me. Their warnings didn't come from a bad place. If anything, it came from the heart.

But the thing is none of them had tried it themselves. So they really had no basis for their cautions.

And my question to you is... Do you have monkeys in your life?

Remember these are not bad people. They're probably your parents who would never hurt a hair on your head. Your siblings, friends or significant other who just want what's best for you. Who want you to get a job and work hard so you can get a good raise, bonus and promotion.

Hey, things are changing. Technology is moving forward. The Internet is booming. Whether or not you want to get on the money train should be your decision, not theirs.

When you recognize these well-meaning monkeys who tell you this won't work, take it with a grain of salt. Have they tried? Do they have this information? Do they own a system?

Well, I do. And I'm going to show you how to use it.

DIGITAL MARKETING EXAMPLE

Mindmap by Tony Buzan

A great book that sells for $19.90 in the bookstore. I recommend it to everyone. It embodies a lifetime of wisdom about learning and how to increase your memory skills using proven techniques.

Stealth Marketing by Jay Abraham

Another great book. But this one sells for US$ 1,000. I've learned so much from this book and it has made me a lot of money. The only difference is that this one is digital.

Why are digital products more expensive than physical ones?

PAIN (does not equal) GAIN

PAIN = PROFIT

Back in 2006 I was in pain. I hated my job. My parents were disappointed in me. I was stuck in traffic for hours on end every day. And my salary was pathetic. With that $51,000 debt hanging over my head I was desperate and in pain.

The pain I felt wasn't exactly physical, though constantly having that burden of debt on my mind definitely wasn't healthy. I was desperate for information on how to make money online.

And Stealth Marketing tapped into that desperation. It reached out to my pain.

So here's the secret to successfully making money online. Take note. Pull out a pen and paper. What you need to do is tap into pain. There. I've said that word five times in a row. If it hasn't gotten through yet, re-read the last 10 sentences.

Now allow me to give you a real-life case study of how I implemented this.

The year was 2009. Farmville was taking over the world. Remember that? The Facebook game that had people so addicted to farming their digital crops on time that jobs were quit and babies abandoned. Even if you weren't actually into that game and playing it, the chances were, your Facebook account was getting hounded by Farmville requests and your newsfeed displayed screenshots of crops. Even if you didn't have a Facebook account you knew about Farmville.

55

While friends of mine who didn't play the game did nothing more than complain about how 'stupid' it was and berate those who were hooked, I looked at things from a different angle. I noticed something that others had overlooked. I saw pain.

And that observation led to one of the most life-changing moments I experienced.

It happened while a friend of mine was telling me how she was exhausted from setting her alarm at 2 am so that she could farm her strawberries. She was sacrificing her sleep for a video game. Her quality of life was affected. In retrospect the situation she put herself in was ridiculous. But that's the thing with addiction. There is no logic. Only pain and instant gratification.

So I took the pain that was obviously in that market and devised a way to not only help alleviate the struggle people like my friend were facing, but to also make money in the process.

I hired a freelance writer for US$350 to create a guide on Farmville. The guide was simple. It taught people how to get more gold coins and plant the best crop rotations. Sounds silly. But it worked.

My guide, Farmville Secrets, was a solution to a very real problem.

It gave people like my friend a way to enjoy the game without affecting her life negatively. Affiliates jumped on and started to promote the guide for me. For every sale they made, they received a commission. Within three days the guide was generating sales of $700 a day. By the end of the first month, I was making $3,500 a day.

And it generated over US$1,000,000 in sales in less than seven months.

57

Now although this was the largest amount of money I had made from a single product at the time, I actually made a number of mistakes. First I set my price at a one-time fee of $17 instead of making it a monthly recurring payment. Imagine what the numbers would be like had I sold that guide for $7/month. I have literally gone YEARS paying for monthly subscriptions of products I've forgotten that I owned. But I'll leave that story for another day...

The second mistake was that I didn't have a sales funnel. Now I know that once you sell something, you should immediately upsell something else. Think about McDonalds and their infamous "Would you like fries with that?" one-liner, which sees more than half the number of customers purchasing the add-on.

Oh well. It still hurts to think about the amount of money I left on the table with Farmville Secrets. But you live, you learn.

And learn I certainly did.

Yet the biggest lesson I received from this was not on marketing, but on life. Before Farmville Secrets I already had around 300 websites under my belt. With all my products combined I was making around $1,000 a day. And I was more than happy to rinse and repeat my automated system to increase that number.

My very first sale, the PayPal notification of $7, taught me, without a doubt, that it was possible to make money online. But I had no idea what the earning potential was until Farmville hit. It completely changed my perspective and opened my eyes to the very real possibility that a guy like me, an almost-college-flunk-out, could generate $10,000 a day from home.

A lot of people said I was just lucky. That I was an overnight success. The inconvenient truth is that being an overnight success takes many late nights. And though I do agree that the Farmville craze, which paralyzed the world for a moment in history, was an anomaly, I don't really believe in 'luck.'

There's a saying that luck is when preparation meets opportunity. I didn't happen to stumble on creating digital products just as Farmville was released. It was an accumulation of years of learning, trial and error, small wins and small losses that led me to that point. As I mentioned, I already had 300 websites before launching Farmville Secrets. I was prepared. It's just that at the time I wasn't completely sure what it was I was preparing for. And I certainly wasn't prepared for that much money!

As for opportunities, I've seen plenty pass people by over and over again. They're either not willing to take a chance or are simply blind to what's staring them in the face. Farmville was a worldwide phenomenon. It affected a lot of people. The opportunity to monetize was there for the taking. And yet, I was the first to create and sell a digital guide about it. I'm not saying

59

this to brag. I'm merely pointing out the importance of being alert, being observant, and most of all seizing every opportunity that comes your way.

When it comes to selling digital information products, look at it as a service that you are providing people. You are not there to rip them off and take their money. You are there to ease whatever pain they are experiencing. You are there to help. And that's why it's important to always deliver on promises and give value to the lives of others.

All profit comes from pain.

Everybody has problems. Successful people don't have any less problems. Successful people just deal with problems different. And everybody is looking for solutions. Be that person to provide that solution. Make the lives of others better, more efficient, faster, smarter, fitter, sexier, happier etc.

Don't think about what you can sell to people, but rather what you can do to help others.

Money is the by-product of providing information people want. Want more money? Begin with the question: "How can I help more people?" or "How can I add more value?"

My father was really proud of his durian farm and he would take a photo every year from conception until we had to sell it back to the government. The following images are his personal photo essay on the growth of the farm. For the first few years, I was too young to follow him there and be part of the family portrait. So instead my older brother, Peng Li, would hold the signs showing the age of the farm. It wasn't until the fifth year that I joined in.

61

Durian Story

A DREAM

Once upon a time, there was a dream......
to grow the "King of Fruits" and produce the
best quality and the most bountiful and
delectable durians in the land.... in the world.

THE DURIANS START TO DROP!

"TEN YEARS BENEATH THE WINDOW SILL, NO ONE ASKED,
ONCE SUCCESS CAME, HEAVEN AND EARTH KNEW"
— OLD CHINESE PROVERB.

THE FIRST BLOOMS

THE FIRST FRUIT

BOUNTIFUL HARVEST D24

RELIABLE BEARER D99

SUCCESS AT LAST

AROUND THE FARM

TOILET ANYONE?

THE DISAPPEARING WATER DURING DROUGHT. THIS WELL
WAS DUG DOWN TO 15 FEET, BUT STILL WAS NOT
SUFFICIENT

THE RESULT

'WHEN IS THIS
GONNA DROP? PENG-LI
SEEMED TO ASK

MEANWHILE JOON
IS DOING A
'JOHN TRAVOLTA'

THE YOUNG TOWKAY WITH THE
OLD BMW

DURIANS GALORE

THE FIRST CROP IN 1988,
6 YEARS AFTER PLANTING
THE KIDS ARE AMAZED THAT
THE DURIANS WERE BORNE
LOWER IN HEIGHT THAN THEM

THE FARMER AND HIS CROP

THE CROP AT 10 YEARS
WAS A BUMPER. BASKETS
OF D24 (RETAILED FROM
RM12 - RM18 PER KILO) ARE
SEEN COLLECTED IN THIS
RAMSHACKLED SHED WHICH
WE OFTEN USED FOR
RELAXATION OR HAVE OUR
LUNCH IN.

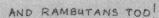

AND RAMBUTANS TOO!

'LET ME GUESS WHAT IT
IS BY TOUCHING. HMMM.....
ITS PROBABLY A RAMBUTAN'
PENG-JOON SEEMS TO SAY

PENG-LI IS BUSY FIXING THE
HARVESTING SHEERS. NOTE HIS
NIKE GUM BOOTS!

'HEH! HEH! I
CAN PASS OFF
AS A RAMBUTAN
TOO' SAYS THE
CHEEKY JOON

THE PUMPHOUSE

THIS PUMPHOUSE HOUSED A 14HP ENGINE COUPLED WITH A WATER PUMP. IT WAS CONSTRUCTED FROM AN OLD RUBBER PROCESSING SHED WITHOUT WALLS WHICH WE SUBSEQUENTLY BUILT IN. NOTICE TOILET SHED ON FAR LEFT. BATHING IS DONE OUTSIDE WITH PAIL (LEFT) AND DRAWING WATER FROM THE RESERVOIR

INSIDE THE PUMPHOUSE: ACTING AS A STORE AS WELL — FOR FERTILISERS, KNAPSACK, WHEELBARROW ETC. NOTE THE POOR QUALITY FINISH OF OUR SELF BUILT WALLS.

BARRICADE TO KEEP SOIL OUT: PENG-LI (NOT VERY HAPPY WITH THE HEAT AND MOSQUITOES) SITTING ON THE SELF-BUILT CEMENT BARRICADE MEANT FOR STOPPING SOIL FROM BEING WASHED INTO THE RESERVOIR

Growing along with Peng-li

WE PHOTOGRAPHED THIS PARTICULAR
D24 TREE WITH PENG-LI EVERY YEAR,
FOR 10 YEARS TO RECORD THEIR
CONCOMITANT DEVELOPMENT

YEAR 1

THE BANANA SHADE IS STILL AROUND.
TRUNKS WERE CUT AND PLACED AROUND
DURIAN TREES FOR MULCH. IRRIGATION
IS ALREADY INSTALLED. THE GROUND
IS STILL BARE

THE TREE IS JUST SLIGHTLY TALLER
THAN PENG-LI

YEAR 2

THE TREE IS NOW TWICE AS
TALL AS PENG-LI. BANANAS
WERE REMOVED AND THE LEGUME
GROUND COVER IS APPARENT IN
THE FOREGROUND

YEAR 3

PENGLI IS GROWING TO BE A STRONG
HEALTHY LAD, SO IS THE DURIAN
TREE.

THE GROUND IS NOW COMPLETELY
COVERED BY A LUSCIOUS GROWTH
OF LEGUME VEGETATION WITH A
SMALL CIRCLE OF BARE GROUND FOR
PLACING FERTILISERS AND FOR
IRRIGATION JETSPRAYS

YEAR 4

NOT A GOOD YEAR FOR THE DURIAN
BECAUSE OF DROUGHT WHICH PROLONGED
FOR 4 MONTHS. OUR WELL DRIED
UP.

THIS TREE HARDLY GREW COMPARED
TO LAST YEAR. NOTICE THE TOP
OF THE CANOPY HAD DRIED UP.
NO DROUGHT FOR PENG-LI THOUGH,
AS HE CONTINUED TO GROW
STRONG AND HEALTHY.

THE TEAM
FROM LEFT : SOON SEE &
JOON (THE ANNUAL VISITORS),
YIN KUAN (FARM MANAGER),
MYSELF AND SOEJINO (HIRED
HAND)

HARVESTING USING CHILD LABOUR
JOON HAVING HIS HANDS FULL

PAID LABOUR : SOEJINO HAVING
HIS WHEEL BARROW FULL

3. SEEING THE DREAM GROW.......

'See the tree how quick its grown..
and Honey it has'nt been too long...
it was'nt there (from 'Honey')

THIS IS A D24 SEEDLING
WHEN IT WAS FIRST PLANTED

THE SAME TREE
10 YEARS LATER.....

YEAR 5

THE TREE RECOVERED
FROM THE DROUGHT BUT
THE BARE TOP IS STILL
EVIDENT.
PENG-LI IS DWARFED BY
THE VIGOUR OF THIS TREE

YEAR 6

PENG-JOON IS FEATURED
WITH PENG-LI FOR THE FIRST
TIME. HE HAS OUTGROWN
THE CRADLE AND DECLARED
'FARM-FIT' TO TRAVEL HERE.
THE TREES ARE GROWING
WITH GUSTO AND A GOOD
CROP WAS OBTAINED THIS
YEAR

YEAR 7

PICTURE PERFECT.... OUR BOYS
POSING WITH THE VIGOROUS DURIAN.
THE INSIDE BRANCHINGS OF THE
TREE HAD DROPPED, GIVING THE
TREE A 'SEE-THROUGH' LOOK. THI
IS AN INDICATION THAT THE TREE
IS MATURE AND READY FOR
BEARING

YEAR 8

THIS TREE FLOWERED AND FRUITED
FAIRLY HEAVILY THIS YEAR. HERE THE
BOYS ARE SHOWING THE CLUSTERS
OF FLOWER BUDS IN EARLY APRIL
FOR THE CROP IN JULY-AUGUST - THE
MAIN FRUITING SEASON IN OUR FARM

PENG-LI IS A TYPICAL TEENAGER NOW,
WEARS REEBOK WHILE JOON, WEARING
AN IRRIGATION COMPANY CAP, IS NOT
NIKE-INCLINED YET.

YEAR 9

THE TREE HAD GROWN SO
MUCH IT JUST WAS NOT
POSSIBLE TO TAKE THE
WHOLE TREE WITHOUT THE
CHILDREN LOOKING LIKE
SPECKS OF SAND. THIS YEAR
WAS A QUIET YEAR BECAUSE
OF THE HEAVY BEARING THE
YEAR BEFORE.
JOON HAS ALSO GROWN -
STARTED TO WEAR LONG PANTS!

YEAR 10

A DECADE OF DURIAN GROWING
OUR PAIR OF CHILDREN ARE
NOW 17 AND 9 RESPECTIVELY

PENG-LI IS READY FOR
UNIVERSITY AND WILL BE
GIVEN A 'DURIAN' SCHOLARSHIP
SOON.

AS PART OF THE 10-YEAR
ANNIVERSARY, THE ORCHARD
PRESENTED US WITH A
WHOPPER-BUMPER HARVEST
OF 30,000 FRUITS!

ALAS, THIS WAS ALSO THE YEAR THE GOVERNMENT ANNOUNCED THE ANNEXATION
OF OUR FARM FOR THE KLIA PROJECT.

THE FARM TODAY

APPROXIMATELY WHERE
THIS TOWER IS STANDING

KL
International
Airport

THE DURIANS ARE LONG GONE. BUT EVEN TODAY AS WE LAND IN KLIA, WE
CAN STILL HEAR THE SOFT WHISPER OF THE DURIAN LEAVES BENEATH THE
WINGS OF THE JETPLANE, REMINISCING THE DREAM OF PLANTING THE
BEST DURIANS ONCE UPON A TIME

- PART II -
SILENT SALES MACHINE

The Silent Sales Machine is a fancy name I came up with for my online money-making system.

(Breakthrough Marketing Tip: Find a tried and tested formula. Slap on a cool name for it. Claim all the credit.)

It's taken me years of trial and error, gone through numerous tweaks and is now perfected.

I call it silent because once it's set up you'll hardly have to touch it. And it will continue to generate your income on autopilot for as long as you want.

Broken down into five parts, all you have to do is follow the steps and you will have your very own online business.

- STEP 1 -

THE LOVECHILD BETWEEN YOUR PASSION AND THE MARKET'S DESIRES

Identifying a Profitable Niche. Maximizing inner passion so you can hit that spot hard every time.

To get started, you first have to forget everything you were ever told growing up:

- You can't make money from a passion.

- You must study something serious that will land you a good job.

- It's great to have hobbies but they will never amount to anything.

- Interests are good on the side but you have to concentrate on 'important' matters.

Look, I've made money from World of Warcraft, Farmville, teeth whitening, piano lessons, Forex and more. And I'm definitely no expert in any of them.

Once you let go of all the stuff you were taught from childhood we can move on.

Ok? Ready?

It's time to find your niche.

Think of your passion. If money were no object, what would you do every day?

Because if you don't love what you're doing, you're going to give up.

Pinpoint your ultimate niche.

Think about what you like, what your passion is, then look at what the market desires, what their needs and wants are. That sweet spot where those two meet is where the money is.

You see, passion can very easily evolve into profit when you find the problem that people are willing to pay to have solved. Some people call me a dreamer or an idealist, but I truly believe that if you live your passion, your life becomes meaningful. And you can turn what you love into wealth.

82

"Man surprised me most about humanity. Because he sacrifices his health in order to make money. Then he sacrifices money to recuperate his health. And then he is so anxious about the future that he does not enjoy the present; the result being that he does not live in the present or the future; he lives as if he is never going to die, and then dies having never really lived."

– DALAI LAMA XIV

Wealth = time x strategy

I believe that everyone will become a millionaire. The question is how long will it take you to get there? 10 years? 30 years? 70 years? The only problem is that people won't live that long.

Often, the Internet is seen as a magic pill to riches.

And I can attest to this. It is a magic pill. The thing is, it's a time-released pill.

It took me nine months to make $7.

The money I made over the next six months from that point equaled that of my then salary.

Another six months later and I was making three times that of my then salary.

Four years down the road and I make in a number of days what it would have taken me one year at my 9-5 job.

That's the power of the Internet. And the key to success is momentum.

DEFINITION: MOMENTUM

A mass in motion; if an object is moving, then it has momentum. The amount of momentum depends on two variables: How much is moving and at what speed.

Keep in mind that momentum is useless if you're heading in the wrong direction. Which is why your inner base must always be aligned with your outer base. The inner base is what drives you personally, while the outer base represents what the market wants.

A lot of people struggle with their inner base. And this comes from years of being told that you'll never amount to anything if you spend all your time _____ (insert your favorite childhood past-time e.g. drawing, singing, gaming, playing sports, dancing etc.) This is bull. Nowadays, people work long hours at a job they hate, to buy things they don't need, to impress people they don't like. But in reality, how often do you really find the time to pick up the paint brush once you're waist deep in the rat race? If you have a hobby or a passion, chances are there are other people who share that interest with you. And those people are always going to want to know how they can _____ (insert your passion in verb form) better, faster, easier...

Never disregard what you love to do as nothing more than a 'hobby'.

Imagine being paid to do what you love every day. That's what we want to focus on.

Only then do you look at whether your passion is what the market desires.

If people are willing to spend money on their hobby, the chances are they'll spend money on information that will show them how to be better at it.

Strength = Passion

Weakness = Poison

85

Always focus on your strength and outsource your weakness.

In my case, my weaknesses include graphics, programming, web design and a whole slew of other skills required to create websites. But I don't let that stop me.

I know my strength is marketing.

Everything else is passed on to someone else. Everything else is outsourced.

Frank Lloyd Wright, an American architect who designed over 1,000 structures and completed 532 works, was once summoned to court.

When asked his occupation he answered he was "the world's greatest architect." His wife Olgivanna was present at the courthouse and reprimanded him for his response. To which he said:

"I had no choice, Olgivanna. I was under oath."

I want you to have that certainty when you pick your niche.

Remember that everybody has experienced pain and problems. Whatever you've lived through, I'm sure there are others who have been through it too.

And it doesn't necessarily have to be physical pain, it could also be to alleviate discomfort or solve an emotional problem.

Think back to my Farmville example.

Farmville.

The pain of wanting to create a better online farm. To get more gold coins. Having to wake up at 4 am to harvest crops on time.

That's a prime example of a problem that's affecting the quality of someone's life. And that's pain.

You already have knowledge and experience that can help others. Tap into that.

There are two groups of people on the Internet:

Browser → Curious

Buyer → Serious & Makes You $$$

87

Your job now is to target the buyers and offer them the convenience of the information that they want at their fingertips.

Now when I set out to write this book I knew I didn't want it to be a textbook. Because they're boring. So I'm not going to teach you about keywords and research and Google and finding your sweet spot.

These are all things that you need to know in order to tap into the market and ka-ching your way to the bank.

I don't know how to tell you how to do these things. I only know how to show you. And since they haven't yet invented a way of incorporating video into physical books, I'm going to direct you to a website where you can watch free step-by-step videos that you can follow to get your online business started today.

www.InternetIncomeIntensive.com

Just head over there to gain full access to my strategies. These are meant only for individuals who are serious about making money online. So I don't want to bore the guys who are only reading this for my awesome stories.

- STEP 2 -

MILKING THE CONTENT COW

*Fresh Unique Content.
Setting up your business and
establishing your brand without
doing any of the hard work.*

O nce you have your niche it's time to dive in and get your website up and running.

I've found that a lot of people stop here because they don't think they have anything new to say. Fresh, unique content. It's a tall order. And I can understand why you may think you don't have the credibility because you're not some PhD expert.

Google CEO Eric Schmidt has this stat to share with you:

"Every two days we create as much information as we did from the dawn of civilization up until 2003."

Any information that you give out will not be new or groundbreaking.

This book is not sharing anything new or groundbreaking.

Making money online is not a new topic.

Internet marketing is not a groundbreaking topic.

Yet what I have that separates me from the seven billion people on this planet is my story.

There is only <u>one</u> you. You are unique. So never fall into the trap of thinking that you don't matter. Because I know that you have experienced something or learned a skill that can help people. And all you need to do is share it.

People often come up to me and say, "But Peng Joon... I'm only a teacher/technician/clerk/waitress/ housewife, what can I possibly offer to other people?" Don't sell yourself short. Look at what you've been through. Look at your own story. What happened to you that made you who you are today? It doesn't have to be hardship or pain. Your day-to-day life is different from every other person on the planet.

Here's a copywriting secret: **Facts tell, stories sell**.

If you try to compete based on content you're never going to win. Not against all the competing content out there. But there's only one you in the whole universe and that's what makes you powerful. Whatever you've gone through, that's powerful.

So I'm sorry to break this to you, but you have no new information to tell the world that it hasn't already heard.

At the end of the day, it's all about how you perceive yourself.

Many people see it this way:

93

That they are one person out of seven billion people... on one planet out of eight planets... in one star system out of 100 billion star systems... in one galaxy out of 100 billion galaxies. How can such a small, insignificant being bring meaning to others?

But I see it this way:

Out of 100 billion galaxies, you are in one galaxy... made up of 100 billion star systems, you are in one star system... of eight planets, you are on one planet... And out of seven billion people, you are one person. Completely unique and unlike any other. And that makes you special.

"You are not just a drop in the ocean.
You are the mighty ocean in the drop."

- RUMI

95

Still wanna be an expert?

Here's what you do to become an expert in your niche. Buy three books about your niche, then read them in a weekend. You will now know more than 95% of the world on that topic.

If you're really hard-up on being an expert then read up and research.

Here's my formula:

Learn → Implement + Gain Experience → Teach

Simply rinse and repeat. Just as Benjamin Franklin says, "Tell me and I forget, teach me and I may remember, involve me and I learn." Only in this case, you're telling, teaching and involving yourself. It's through the act of *doing* that you'll grow both as a person as well as in your knowledge.

But here's an insider secret:

People don't pay to listen to experts. People pay to listen to people who they relate to, who have real life experience and who have overcome the problems that they are currently facing.

Experts are a dime a dozen. So put away the belief that you're not an expert and that people wouldn't care to listen to what you have to say.

I am not the richest Internet marketer in the world. But my students come to me because they relate to what I have to say. They trust me because they see a lot of themselves in me. They know my story and it often reflects theirs.

It's your personal angle on things that will interest others. It's what you bring to the table that matters. And the reason why I don't get writer's block is because I always have an opinion on everything. And that's what I share with people. Even if they don't want to listen.

97

What I'm trying to say is, content itself doesn't do anything.

"Content is king but marketing is queen and that bitch runs the house."

- GARY VAYNERCHUK

Always focus on the marketing. Because that's where the money is.

When it comes to content, you want to be an authority.

It's like being the head honcho of your tribe. Everyone comes to you for your insights, information and opinion. When you reach this level, your marketing efforts will actually be much easier as your loyal customers will be the ones spreading the word about you for free.

But before we jump ahead to the finish line, let's talk about getting off the starting block.

99

Now, if you're not a natural writer or you find the task mundane and boring, don't worry.

Because later on I'll show you a way to consistently deliver great content through your website without having to write a single word.

It's still important that you understand how this works so that you remain in full control of your brand and positioning.

WHY IS CONTENT IMPORTANT?

Now I know I just went on about how marketing is more important than content, and while that's true, you can't put up an empty website and expect people to stick around and stare at a blank screen.

There are three main components to a website:

- URL/Hosting (that's all the www. stuff)

- Graphics/Design (making things pretty)

- Content (stuff that people read)

Many budding online entrepreneurs make the mistake of thinking that design is the focus of a good website. And while it can influence the success of a website, content trumps it.

In fact there are a huge number of sites I frequent which are ugly as hell but have some of the most useful and interesting information out there.

Because as concerned as people are about aesthetics, all it really comes down to in the end is the content.

"It's the inside that counts, not the outside…"

Actually, technically the insides are, well... the technical things that come with a website. But you know what I mean.

SETTING UP YOUR BUSINESS

The great thing about starting an online business is that you don't have to cough up ridiculous amounts of cash to get it off the ground. There's no waiting around for bank loan approvals or scouring your contact list to beg, borrow or steal in order to gather capital.

With an online business, all you need is a website.

And in order to get a website you only need two things.

1. **Your domain**

2. **Your hosting**

A domain is the name of your website that people will type into the address bar i.e. **www.PengJoon.com**, which is my personal blog; pengjoon is my domain name that I purchased for around $10.

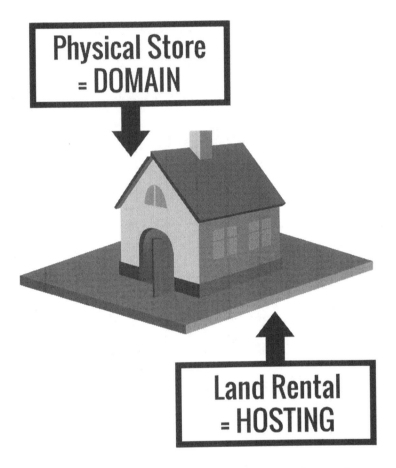

If you imagine a domain as a physical store, then hosting is simply the rental of the land where you place your store. And on the Internet, that 'rental' is about $10 a month.

Honestly, these two tasks take less than 15 minutes to set up and by the end of it you'll have your own website, in your control, to do whatever you want with. Including generating an income.

It sounds too good to be true doesn't it?

How can 15 minutes of 'work' create an online empire?

It can, and that's really all it takes to set up your own business online. And that's why I absolutely love the Internet with its endless possibilities.

In order for you to get the most out of this book and my system, just head over to **www.InternetIncomeIntensive.com** and enter your email address in the box provided. From there you'll gain full access to all the videos that I created specifically for you on how to get these steps done. If you're a little confused, stop reading now and go get your online business set up and ready to go!

That way you won't get left behind and when you turn to the next chapter – we'll both be on the same page. Literally and figuratively.

The videos I've prepared come with step-by-step instructions for you to follow at your own pace.

SEARCH ENGINES LOVE CONTENT

Back when I first started Internet marketing, it was the norm to 'game the system' and crazy easy to get a website ranked in the first page of Google within hours of it going live.

Internet marketers are obsessed with getting their website on the first page of Google because the vast majority of people will click on the first result they see. Stats differ here and there, but I have seen evidence that the 1st position in Google receives 53% of clicks.

One of the ways I would get that top rank was to stuff a bunch of keywords into one website that I wanted to rank for, and buy backlink pyramids. (You don't really need to know what this means because it's all really shady and scammy and will end up damaging your reputation and website very quickly!)

But in 2006, all these dirty tricks worked and it was like printing money every day.

Thankfully Google introduced their algorithms, Panda and Penguin, which slapped the shit out of all those sites, including mine.

The reason I say "thankfully" is because I am truly grateful that it happened, though a lot of marketers still bitch about it constantly.

Google cleaned up the web so dirty tricks no longer worked. Sites that showed up on the first page of the search results got there because they were relevant and actually provided content that helped web users. And what was it that got them in that awesome position?

Content.

With good content you never have to worry about new algorithms and updates clamping down on you.

105

Just remember this: Search engines are content driven and strive to serve their users better by delivering great web results for every search. Which brings me to my next point…

GIVE QUALITY CONTENT

Your aim is to target a human being. Not a search engine.

So provide quality content that answers questions your visitors have, give them information that is interesting and tips that are useful.

Because you are reading this I am assuming you are a human being. My best advice is to write like a human being, for other human beings.

Grammar and spelling are secondary.

Write the way you speak. You're not producing a text book. You're simply sharing awesome information with your personal spin on things.

TARGET YOUR AUDIENCE

Before producing any content, focus on who your target audience is. This comes back to drilling down into your niche and really identifying the market that lives there.

By understanding the keywords that your ideal audience is searching for, you can create content that caters to it.

Take for example the gaming niche that I started out in.

The content that I put up would include strategies to completing a game in the fastest, most efficient way possible with extra cheats and tips and advice. It would be pretty stupid to create content on the background of the game developers, the history of PC games, the evolution of gamers and whatever.

People who are looking to purchase game guides don't care about that stuff.

So consider what your audience cares about... and write about those things.

107

A PICTURE SAYS A THOUSAND WORDS...

So how many words is a video worth? Video marketing and video blogging are awesome for a lot of reasons. And I'm going to come back to them throughout this book.

In fact, I'm going to get started right now on the next page.

USING VIDEOS AS CONTENT

If you're not much of a writer, or generally have no interest in it whatsoever, then videos could be your calling.

Honestly it takes me an hour to write what I could just say in three minutes.

But then, I'm not much of a writer.

Vlogging is a powerful way of adding value to your website and keeping your visitors engaged and happy. Just use the tips I provided in the previous chapter and instead of writing out a blog post, record yourself sharing the information and post that up instead.

Now for the ridiculously lazy people out there, if this also feels like a chore, I have a secret method to creating great content.

It's by using other people's videos to pass off as your own.

And don't worry. It's not some renegade douchebag move. It's absolutely legal and ethical.

But before we get into that...

WHY IS VIDEO SO POWERFUL?

Statistics have shown that video content is 53 times more likely to rank on the first page of Google than its text-only counterpart.

Furthermore over 50% of users will click on the first link of the first page in the search results, compared to a mere 15% who click on the second link.

So imagine what your chances are of generating any organic traffic if your content shows up on the second page...

WHY DOES VIDEO RANK SO WELL?

Google owns YouTube. So videos on YouTube receive preferential treatment from Google.

There's no need to scoff at this. That's silly and petty. Instead, take advantage of the situation and be at the receiving end of this special treatment.

BENEFITS OF VIDEO CONTENT

1. Search Engine Optimization

Get a higher rank in the search engines so your website shows up on the first page. And of course this means much more traffic heading in your direction.

2. Building relationships

Video develops your brand and helps build that all-important relationship between you and your ideal audience. By speaking directly to them they get to know your face, your voice, your mannerisms and who you really are. This puts a face to a name and allows your customers to know with whom they're doing business.

3. Establishing yourself as an authority

By creating video content that educates your target audience you become the face of the industry. Just take Gordon Ramsey or Jamie Oliver for example. They're not the best chefs in the world. But because they engage their audience on video, they immediately become viewed as authorities in their niche. Capiche?

4. Converting visitors to buyers

Video has proven to increase sales substantially over text-only offers. I know this first hand. Sales videos are a must when it comes time to create your sales letter.

Now back to the secret method of creating killer video content the lazy way.

I do this by using other people's hard work and passing it off as my own. Now don't go stealing copyrighted material. That's not cool. And it'll get you sued.

There's a stealth technique that only a handful of people know.

It includes exploitation and glory. Yet is completely ethical and will never get you into trouble with anyone.

Within minutes you'll have amazing content on your website that will attract visitors and you don't have to come up with a single creative thought. No work involved.

Interested in knowing what it is?

All you have to do is head over to **www.InternetIncomeIntensive.com** and I'll show you with my free video tutorials.

- STEP 3 -

GETTING PEOPLE EXCITED OVER SOMETHING THEY DIDN'T KNOW THEY WANTED

*Product Promotion.
Getting the word out in more ways
than one and achieving success
by piggybacking on the
shoulders of giants.*

Although this chapter is about getting people excited over something they didn't know they wanted, you can't go around promoting a product you haven't created yet. So I should probably have called this step Product Creation. But whatever.

Creating a product really isn't all that difficult.

In fact, aside from the first few World of Warcraft guides I put out at the start, I've never really created anything myself.

As in, the products that I launch are written and created by other people who I've paid to write and create products for me.

Make sense?

Anyway, here's my product creation template.

1. What is it?

2. Why is it important?

3. How to do it.

The first two parts should take up less than 20% of your product, while the focus lies in the 'how' part.

For example, the product could be How To Be Sexy.

And your guide on how to be sexy would be something like this:

Being sexy is when other people find you attractive and want to have sexy time with you.

It's important because if you're not sexy, people will not want to have sexy time with you and that's depressing.

To be sexy you should follow these 5 steps:

1. Practice your *blue steel* look in the mirror until it's perfect then showcase it to people you want to find you sexy.

2. Watch the movie *Zoolander* if you don't understand the *blue steel* reference.

3. Re-watch the movie *Zoolander* if you *did* understand the *blue steel* reference because it's sexy.

4. Dance like Usher.

5. Hang out with sexy people.

Yeah. I wouldn't try selling that. But hopefully you get my drift.

That's all you need to have a product of your own. Of course you should add actual value to the information you're sharing. People are, after all, paying you money for it. And never forget that at the core of our business, the goal is to help others and ease their pain.

Still unsure about creating your own product?

Fuck perfection.

119

It's a digital product. Not a masterpiece. It's not about creating your masterpiece today, it's about putting oil on the canvas every day.

The great thing about digital products is you can always go back and edit them. The important thing is to get it done and into the marketplace.

I started writing this book in 2006. Yes, this exact book in your hands right now.

I'd start, then stop and edit. Start again, go back and edit. I wanted it to be perfect. And that need for perfection paralyzed me to the point where I stopped starting and just stopped.

120

I hired a ghostwriter. Paid $10,000 for it. Hated it because it wasn't authentic enough. Started from scratch again. 2008. Didn't do anything. 2009. Re-did the whole thing…

There are five versions of this book.

Version 1 is 300++ pages long.

There is a book in everyone. But the only reason it doesn't get published is because of perfection. Full stop.

That's when I realized that perfection sucks. And no matter how 'perfect' you get anything to be, there's still gonna be haters hating on you and your work. So fuck perfection.

Hence this awesome book that you are currently enjoying so very much.

Now my first digital product was a 17-page eBook which I sold for $7.

Once you have your digital product set up and ready to be sold, you need to write a sales page that will do the selling for you. This requires copywriting which can make or break the success of your product.

I'm not here to teach you about copywriting. That would be a whole other book on the power of words. Which doesn't sound like a whole lot of fun for me to write.

So let's focus on the marketing aspect of it all.

121

THIS CHAPTER IS REALLY ABOUT PRODUCT PROMOTION

When it comes to promoting your product, there are a ton of different strategies out there that work at varying degrees of effectiveness.

I WANT TO TELL YOU ABOUT THREE THINGS.

1. Affiliate marketing

2. Email marketing

3. Joint ventures

In a nutshell, affiliate marketing is when a marketer promotes someone else's product. And when they make a sale, they receive a commission.

Every product I created was placed on an affiliate marketing platform called Clickbank, and was open to any affiliate marketers to promote. Back when I first started out, I offered a 50% commission for every sale an affiliate made.

By doing this I pretty much let other people promote my products for me. And all I had to do was sit back and receive my half of the profit every time someone else sold my product. You may be thinking that 50% is way too much to give to other people, and far too little to receive after all your hard work. But here's the thing. Creating a product and slapping a price tag on it is easy. The hard part is getting the word out amid all the noise on the Internet and getting the attention of potential buyers. That's what marketing is all about. So by offering a high commission payout, I'm actually giving incentive for other people to do the hard work for me. And I still get half the profit.

That being said, one of the most life-changing moments I encountered was when I experienced the power of email marketing first-hand.

123

The first thing I do every morning is open my email and check my sales for the day.

Back at the start of my online career I was averaging one to three sales daily. That brought in $37-$100 a day.

One morning I looked at my inbox and my jaw dropped to the ground. I was certain there had been a mistake. My product had totaled $45,000 worth of sales overnight.

Holy crap.

What happened was Brian Kopp, an authority in World of Warcraft, had picked up on my product and sent out one email promoting it to his list of subscribers.

After his 50% commission was paid out, I made $22,500 overnight. Doing absolutely nothing. Well, not nothing. I was sleeping. I made $22,500 sleeping.

That was more money than I had made in the last two years at my day job. Made overnight. While I slept.

I know I'm repeating myself in different ways. I got it from my mum. But I want you to understand the power of this.

I got paid to sleep.

By having an established name promote for me, I got massive huge traffic and conversions.

The huge traffic came from the fact that Brian Kopp was incredibly well-known and had a lot of fans and followers. At that time anyway. Because of this, these people subscribed to his email list to get more material, insights and promotions from him.

And the crazy conversions were a result of his reputation as a trustworthy source of top-notch information.

All he had to do was say, "I approve this product, buy it." And they did.

Well, I'm sure he wrote it in a much more eloquent way. But that's beside the point.

The point is leveraging off an established authority like Brian Kopp is a form of a joint venture.

On my end, I created a product.

On his end, he promoted it to his email list.

125

And in the end the result was $22,500 in each of our bank accounts.

Now one of the hidden gems in this strategy is that not only will you make sales through affiliates, but you also receive the contact details of the customers who purchased your product. So you essentially make money and build an email list of your own. As this system repeats, your list will grow and eventually you can promote directly to your target market through email marketing, cutting out the middleman. 100% profit in your pocket. Powerful right?

After that very fateful morning, after I peeled my dead carcass off the floor, I realized one thing.

Affiliate Marketing + Email Marketing + Joint Ventures = Da Shit.

And that's somewhat been my secret formula to making money online.

If you'd also like to get paid to sleep, then visit **www.InternetIncomeIntensive.com** to watch me live so that I can show you how to do it. Trust me when I say it's a crapload easier to show you this stuff than it is to write about it.

DEFINITION: AFFILIATE MARKETING

Promoting other people's products and cashing in by receiving commissions for every successful sale.

DEFINITION: EMAIL MARKETING

Getting people to sign up to your email newsletter then sending them a bunch of email that will build a relationship with them so they like you, then selling stuff to them to make money.

DEFINITION: JOINT VENTURE

Teaming up with a person (or several people) to make craploads of cash by leveraging off their name.

127

YOUR NETWORK IS YOUR NET WORTH

At the time of writing this book, I have had a billion gazillion Clickbank #1 product launches. If you're unsure of what that means, basically there are thousands of digital products in Clickbank's marketplace. Their most competitive category is e-business and e-marketing.

The products that I created and launched in that niche made it to #1 by grossing the highest sales.

And it's not because they were really awesome products, like I mentioned previously:

Content is King but Marketing is Queen... and that bitch runs the house.

Yup, it was the marketing that got those products selling like hot cakes. (Cold cakes taste pretty damn good too. The saying should just be "selling like cakes." I like cake. Once when I was craving chocolate cake I went out and bought the biggest five-layer chocolate cheese cake I could find and ate it. And it was cold.)

So how did I manage to launch #1 products?

Through joint ventures.

You see at the end of the day it's not what you know but who you know that will make or break your business. I guess it's like any business.

It takes time to build relationships with the top guns of any industry. But if you do it correctly, you're going to have a super lucrative career forever.

MEET SOME OF MY PARTNERS IN PROFIT:

Joel Bauer is the mentor to the mentors. The guru to the gurus. The master to the masters. With over 30 years on platforms presenting and closing, Joel has created a proven system to generate significant revenue both on and off stage. His client list includes Motorola, Shell, Mitsubishi, Disney and more. Also, he's designed turn-key closing presentations for top dogs like Mark Victor Hansen, Robert Alan and Anthony Robbins to name a few.

Joel has been featured in the *Wall Street Journal*, appeared on CNN, ABC, NBC, MTV, etc. There are just not enough pages in this book to list down his numerous achievements.

I went from learning with him to launching products together.

To date, Alex Mandossian has generated over $233 million in sales for clients and partners via e-marketing including teleseminars, radio, TV and the Internet. His vast clientele includes NYU, Trim Spa and Dale Carnegie Training to name a few. He knows his stuff.

Alex is a world-renowned speaker who has shared the stage with guys like Donald Trump, Les Brown, T. Harv Eker and more. I could gush over him all day but the point I'm trying to make is that he's already a master. He's established and able to make more than enough money on his own.

Yet I found a way to add value and in 2012 we collaborated and launched a huge digital product. It was called Membership Sites Blueprint which is a complete A-Z blueprint that covers all the important aspects of membership site building. It taught people how to generate a recurring stream of passive income from a single product. And within a week it shot up to the #1 rank in the Clickbank marketplace.

133

I met John Chow at a seminar we both happened to attend where we sat next to each other. He's a world famous blogger who was able to monetize his blog and go from zero to earning $40,000 a month on passive income. And he did it working only two hours a day. His blog, John Chow dot Com, is synonymous with the term 'make money online' and is ranked number 16 on the AdAge Power 150 list and number one on the list of the Top 50 Canadian Internet Marketing Blogs. John currently has 300,000 unique visitors a day and is the founder and CEO of his own company. Again, there is so much more to this guy than I have time to write.

After meeting him at the seminar, we kept in contact and to date have launched multiple bestselling membership sites and projects together, solidifying both our reputations in the industry, making a lot of money, and helping many people empower themselves through the information we give away.

Through John, I met Shoemoney.

Jeremy Schoemaker, better known as Shoemoney, is best known for earning $130,000 in a month from Google AdSense. But there's a hell of a lot more on his shelf of achievements. Shoe is the pioneer of online ringtone downloads and the man behind the launch of AuctionAds, an eBay affiliate marketing service, which later sold to Media Whiz for a massive undisclosed sum. A super blogger, serial-online-multimillionaire entrepreneur, marketer and author, Shoe has done it all.

In 2013 we partnered and created Shoe-In Money. Another bestseller.

135

And so my network grows.

Now I don't just sit around on my ass all day waiting for intros. And if you're planning on doing that you're not going to get very far. I went out and created opportunities for myself. Yes, a number of them landed on my lap. But not until I put in all the grunt work first, which allowed these opportunities to blossom and appear to me.

You have to get noticed.

Now that I'm in a position where many people are consistently approaching me to JV with them, I see both sides of the story. From the eye of the proposer and the eye of the proposee. What's the right word for that? I have no idea.

Here's the number one mistake that people make.

They approach people and beg them to promote their crappy product. In return they promise a commission for the sales they make.

That ain't enough, man.

Remember that you are leveraging off someone's name and reputation. They've made a ton of money in their own right. They have people hanging on their every word. By promoting your product they're giving their stamp of approval and telling the world that they vouch for you.

So if it turns out that your product really is crap, then it not only looks bad on you, but worse on them.

What I'm trying to say is you have everything to gain, while they have everything to lose. You have to make sure you know what you're doing.

That's one thing.

Another thing is that these guys are receiving hundreds of proposals a day. You need to stand out in order for them to give you a second thought.

The best way to get noticed is to go out on a limb and help them first before even suggesting a partnership. Promote their products, make them a hell of a lot of money and work on building a relationship with them.

When you have their attention, remember that you're still a small fry. Offer your services, let them know what's in it for them, and then do ALL the work.

They've already worked damn hard to get their name and rep to what it is.

So don't ask them to do a thing.

Remember the awesome Brian Kopp story I just told you? Yeah, that's what you want for yourself. And he didn't do anything except send one email out. $22,000 overnight.

That's the power of joint ventures.

Now, many of these opportunities came up not because I happened to be in the right place at the right time. But because I made sure I was in the right place, I made it the right time and I was prepared.

Since then, I have either met, shared the stage or worked with these leaders, luminaries and legends.

But first... let me take a selfie

Speaking with Tony Robbins @ Total Success Australia Tour

With Robert Kiyosaki, author of #1 Bestseller, *Rich Dad Poor Dad* @ South Africa Tour

Exploring Taj Mahal, India with Les Brown, the world's #1 motivation speaker

With Frank Kern, highest paid internet consultant @ War Room Mastermind

With Ryan Deiss, CEO of Digital Marketer @ DM HQ

Sharing the stage with Brendon Burchard, 3x #1 NY Times Bestselling Author @ NAC KL

Speaking with Brian Tracy, personal development trainer & legend @ Chennai, India

With the king of #hustle, Gary Vaynerchuk

On multi country world tour with top marketing strategist, Jay Abraham

Speaking with Nick Vuijicic; No arms, no legs, no limits

"Rich Dad, Real Dad"

DEFINITION: TRAFFIC

Traffic is basically people. The higher your traffic, the more visitors you have coming to your website.

- STEP 4 -

REELING IN IDEAL CUSTOMERS

Get Targeted Traffic.
Advice you should absolutely never
follow and legit techniques that
will bring in the cash flow.

There are many strategies and tactics to generate traffic. What a lot of people don't understand is why they need traffic. So let's spell it out Sesame Street style:

It doesn't matter if you have the best website in the entire omniverse, if no one ever sees it you'll never make a cent.

Now that we're nearing the end of this life-changing book, I imagine that you might be feeling a little overwhelmed with all the information I've been so generously giving away to you. And you may be thinking that although all this money I'm making sounds awesome and that you'd like to have it too, you feel like it's a hell of a lot of learning and work and shit that you have to go through to reach my position.

And you know what?

You're absolutely right.

It is a damn lot of learning and work and shit that you'll have to go through.

But here's the thing.

Your income can only grow to the extent that you do, and the only way to grow is to be outside your comfort zone.

Sounds corny because it is corny. But it's true.

"YOUR INCOME CAN ONLY GROW TO THE EXTENT THAT YOU DO, AND THE ONLY WAY TO GROW IS TO BE OUTSIDE YOUR COMFORT ZONE"

Case Study – Yours Truly

My whole life I've dreaded the thought of speaking in public.

When I started seeing success with this whole make-money-online thing, I got excited and wanted to share what I'd learned with others.

Because I know what it's like to be stuck in rush hour traffic for two hours going to a job you hate, every damn day. To work your ass off for some douchebag and getting shit for pay. Mundane. Boring. Uninspiring. And yet… comforting.

There's no fear of failure when you don't try. There's no risk involved. Everything is cushy and safe, albeit depressing as fuck.

But you won't get anywhere being cushy and safe.

149

I took a risk when I quit my crappy job and jumped into Internet marketing head first with no safety net. It wasn't easy. I've had a lot of failures and plenty more to come I'm sure. I power through it and learn and adapt and improve.

A setback is a setup for a comeback.

And as my bank account grew so did my desire to share what I knew with others.

Friends, family, acquaintances and strangers all living in miserable comfort. Looking for a way out. Wanting to actually learn how to earn some pocket money or a full-blown income online. I had that knowledge. But I couldn't bring myself to speak in public.

The very thought of it made me physically sick to my stomach.

Then I realized that not only was I missing out on a massive opportunity to help others, but those people were losing out by not getting to the information in my big head.

I made it my responsibility to share.

Because I knew I could make a difference in people's lives.

I am totally blowing my own horn. But goddamn it's true.

So I signed up for various speaking seminars and learnt how to give public talks. I watched great speakers on stage and emulated them. I studied and practiced and prepared to face my fear.

One day the opportunity arose for me to take the stage and speak to a room of people.

151

I spent three weeks preparing for that workshop. For eight hours a day I would go over research, structure, content, pronunciation and more. The night before I was scheduled to talk I couldn't sleep.

I puked twice.

When I finally took the stage, I had a pile of notecards in one hand that would put the *Lord of the Rings* to shame. I read each word. There were 1,000 people in the room. At the end of it, there was no relief.

Because out of those 1,000 people, I only got three 'conversions.' That means only **three** people got anything out of my talk and decided to buy what I was selling. That's a 0.3% conversion rate.

It was an utter failure.

I wanted crawl into a hole and turn into a cabbage.

But the words of Les Brown followed me. "If you can look up, you can get up." So I persevered.

I later returned to that stage and crushed it. And I've been crushing it ever since and have done consistent sold out events in now over 20+ countries around the world.

"Every master was once a disaster."

- T. HARV EKER

And that's absolutely true.

People don't believe me when I tell them that I used to suck at public speaking. But I was truly awful. I have recordings of my speaker trainings. It's humiliating to even think about it, let alone put it down on paper. Publicly berated and crushed. Only to come out stronger and better on the other side.

I stepped out of my comfort zone and was met with an unresponsive crowd that stared at me like I had just wasted an hour of their lives that they'd never get back.

But did I let that stop me?

Fuck no.

I just went back to the drawing board and signed up for more seminars and programs. And I continued speaking in public. Again and again.

Just like many things in life, public speaking is a learnable skill. You don't have to be born with a gift. You don't have to be a natural at anything. You can learn it. It may come harder or easier to you as compared to others. But at the core of it, you have to want it enough to achieve it. And that rings true not just with Internet marketing, but with any venture you embark on in life.

Perseverance pays off.

Now my signature seminar, Internet Income Intensive, boasts thousands of alumni who are earning money online based on the techniques that I taught them.

I did good.

And I'm proud of that.

If we were to give up every time we fell, then we'd all still be crawling on the floor like babies.

The thing about kids is that they don't fear rejection or humiliation. They aren't confined to the standards society sets on adults. When a baby tries to walk, stumbles and falls, people help them up and applaud their efforts.

That mindset is lost to us now. And it shouldn't be.

Because if you really want to be good at something, you have to be willing to be bad at it first. And that's a problem that most people face. They don't want to look bad.

So if you want to make a difference, whether in your life or others, don't allow yourself to be comfortable.

Step out. Get uncomfortable. Because only then will you be able to grow. And that's when your income will follow.

BACK TO TRAFFIC AND THE BENEFITS OF HAVING IT:

- More money

- More sales

- More clickthroughs

- More subscribers to your email list

- More exposure

- More referrals

- Higher chance of beating your competitors

- Higher chance of visitors sharing your content

- Potential to improve search engine ranking

- Less need to advertise

There are tons of ways to generate traffic. The most basic are categorized under paid traffic or free traffic. As a Malaysian I understand more than anyone that free always sounds awesomeballs. That's why I created this:

157

A DEFINITIVE TABLE ON WHY PAID TRAFFIC IS WAY BETTER THAN FREE TRAFFIC:

PAID TRAFFIC	FREE TRAFFIC
FAST	SLOW
• Get laser-targeted visitors who are interested in your offer on your website immediately. • Collect data to see how successful your campaign was. • Tweak and perfect to repeat repeatedly.	• Approximately six months to forever before you see results, if any. • Even then you can't be sure what worked and what didn't because it's impossible to track. • Visitors are far less targeted and you could end up with a bunch of hobos trolling the Internet landing on your site by chance.
MEASURABLE	NON-MEASURABLE
• Track your traffic to see where it came from to a specific dollar amount. • Calculate EXACTLY how much money you are actually making. • If you make a lot, do it again. • If you don't make any, stop doing it and do something else then track that to see how much money you're making.	• You have a higher chance of success licking your elbow while sneezing with your eyes open than trying to track free traffic. • i.e. you'll have no idea whether the methods you used worked or not.

PAID TRAFFIC	FREE TRAFFIC
PREDICTABLE	UNPREDICTABLE
• Paid traffic is GUARANTEED. • Once you find a method that works you only need to duplicate it over and over and over and over and over and over and over and over and over again.	• Totally hit-and-miss. • No guarantee whatsoever. • You have zero control over everything.
SCALABLE	ONE-DIMENSIONAL
• You can start small. • After calculating your earnings, you can scale up. Buy big. And make much more money.	• You can't go bigger. • Implement a free traffic strategy and that's it. • No possible way to make more money at the click of a button.

But you really need to know what you're doing.

Early in my career when I first tried out Google AdWords, I made the mistake of going in with blind arrogance confidence. I paid $2,000 for an ad to be displayed then went for lunch.

[Do you know that I hold a personal record of eating 100 Alaskan crab legs in a Vegas buffet?]

Post-lunch I came back to find my $2,000 had been burned. I got 3 sales.

Because I made one tiny newbie mistake...

I forgot to check a box.

That's why you've got to know what you're doing with paid traffic.

TRAFFIC GENERATION TECHNIQUES THAT ARE OUTDATED AND THAT YOU SHOULD ABSOLUTELY NOT USE EVER

At the beginning of my Internet marketing expedition I went the blackhat route. That means I gamed the system and used a bunch of awesomely frowned-upon strategies to get traffic and make sales.

One such tactic that I'm personally very proud of is spamming MySpace.

Back then, MySpace was huge and Facebook was a tiny insignificant speck.

I would go to MySpace adder and look for friends who were friends with World of Warcraft. Then I would use this software that automatically

160

adds them to my friend list. Muahahaha. After that, I'd send them messages like, "Have you checked out this new guide?" [Insert link to said guide that makes moo-lah for me every time someone purchases.]

I averaged five sales a day. Not bad. I was happy. And I tell myself those people were happy too because they got an awesome guide out of it.

Then six days later my account got shut down.

Have you heard of a Google slap?

I used to set up 'sniper sites'. These are one-page websites that have around three posts, packed with one keyword. With that same keyword in the URL. Then I'd usually pay about $5 to have thousands of links set back to that one website. You see, the more links you have coming to your site, the higher your search engine rank. And back then it was really easy to rank as the first result for that keyword on Google just by doing these things. Totally non-legit by the way. Super blackhat to the max.

The result would be a crazy amount of traffic and sales.

161

In February 2011, Google released an algorithm called Panda, which went around the Net murdering affiliate sites. This cyber-genocide is referred to as a slap. I received multiple slaps. My personal email is still banned by Google. I tried to get unbanned. Called Google's support staff in India. They talked me round in circles.

So I opened a new Google account. And now I use that.

My lawyers strongly advised me not to tell you that but fuck it.

162

A SUPER LEGIT TRAFFIC GENERATION METHOD THAT WORKS AND THAT YOU NEED

List Building.

When you have your own email list, you only need to blast out one email to your subscribers with a link back to your website (or any site for that matter) and they'll be there in droves.

On top of that, an email list is your personal ATM. When you have one, you can send out one promotional email and get tens, if not hundreds of thousands of dollars of profit in return.

Refer to the previous chapter to re-read my awesome Brian Kopp story.

But there's a hell of a lot more to it than that.

And to find out the 'more' it will require me to use terminology like autoresponder, ethical bribe, squeeze page, geo-targeting, opt-in box, swipes, solo ads and swaps.

DEFINITION:

Autoresponder, ethical bribe, squeeze page, geo-targeting, opt-in box, swipes, solo ads and swaps.

Rather than me telling you what all this means, I feel it'd be much easier if I just show you. So if you're interested in seeing how to grow your very own email list that will generate massive amounts of traffic and cash, then just head over to **www.InternetIncomeIntensive.com** where I've set up a complete video series that you can follow step-by-step for free.

I've included an entire module dedicated to building a money-making email list. This includes easy-to-follow instructions and walkthrough videos. And remember, this is all yours free of charge! No credit card details required whatsoever.

- STEP 5 -

Automate. Created and perfected, now duplicated many times over. Complete your personal money machine and gain financial freedom.

One of my early online money-making endeavors was to offer SEO services. I'd complete three websites a day and my clients would pay me $300 a pop. That's not bad for a 23-year old college-almost-dropout.

It was during a family gathering over lunch that I met up with a very successful uncle of mine. He's the CEO of a major corporation. I (kinda) bragged to him about how well my business was doing. And then he asked me this one question which turned everything around:

"How much money are you making right now?"

I paused for a bit. Then stated that obviously I wasn't making anything because I was having lunch with the family.

He looked at me and said that although he was at the same lunch, his business was still churning out profits. He didn't need to physically be working in order to make money.

So here's the lesson: **You will never be rich if you continue to trade your time for money.**

My uncle's business was fully automated and continued to run even when he wasn't around.

This is a concept that was lost even to my parents. Many people believe that in order to make more money, they need to work more.

Think about this: If the amount of money we earn was directly proportional to the number of hours we put in, then why is it that people like Donald Trump, Sir Richard Branson and Oprah Winfrey can be billionaires? Do they sleep less? Or did they hack into the space-time continuum to give themselves more hours? Of course not. Though that would be awesome.

Everyone is given the same 24 hours a day. So if your focus is to work more to earn more, how much more can you possibly give?

What you need to do is build a money machine.

169

Always remember that money works for you, you don't work for money.

HOW TO BUILD A MONEY MACHINE

The beauty of this business is that the sale of digital products runs on autopilot.

Once you've set it up, you can leave it online forever and ever and people can visit your site years down the line and still purchase it.

Remember that buffet service I talked about? That's automation. That's your money machine.

Never fall into the trap of thinking that if you want to make more money you have to work more hours.

There's only so much one person can do. So for you to really scale up and automate your business, you have to outsource.

DEFINITION: OUTSOURCING

Getting other people to do your work for you.

With outsourcing you are leveraging off the skills of other people so that you can have more time to concentrate on:

1. The things you're good at.

2. The things you enjoy doing.

If I didn't outsource, I'd be chained to my laptop all day working on sites, writing content, struggling through graphic design and learning how to program.

Newsflash: I am not a writer. I am not a web designer. I am not a programmer.

I am a marketer.

Again, I'm repeating myself because I really want it to be clear that you do not need to know these things in order to successfully start and run a profitable online business. All you need is the marketing know-how. And that is exactly what I'm showing you based on my own experience.

There are tons of outsourcing websites out there where you can hire contractors inexpensively.

This is the process:

1. Sign up and become a member of an outsourcing site.

2. Post a job description.

3. Look through the applicants.

4. Shortlist candidates, interview, hire the best.

5. Manage them as they do your work for you while you spend the rest of your time doing awesome stuff.

6. When the job is done, pay your contractor by sending payment through the secure outsourcing site where you hired them.

The fact is I can set up a website, put up content, update it every day, drive traffic to it and build my email list. But it's going to take a lot of my time. And if I want to do it all myself then there's no possible way for me to own my current 500 websites…

That's why I have a team that looks after all that for me. And I just concentrate on other things while my inbox gets spammed by PayPal payment notifications.

It sounds cocky and obnoxious. But to be honest, as long as you have a system set up, you truly will be making money on autopilot and making sales from all over the world at any time of day and night. That's the beauty of the Internet. It doesn't close for business. You don't have to pay staff to keep your store open and greet customers. You don't need to stress over warehousing or inventory.

173

These digital products are created once and downloaded millions of times. No wear and tear. No expiry date.

How much is your time worth?

Remember at the start I told you to readjust your money blueprint, well now I need you to readjust your time blueprint. Because if you're waking up early every day to get stuck in rush hour traffic so you can go to a job you don't like for eight hours, only to get stuck in rush hour traffic on the way home where you

have to sleep early to repeat the process all over again…
Well, it's time you value your time. It's a resource that
can never be replaced. Ever.

And you could replace all the words I just wrote
with an online business and it would be the same
outcome if you insisted on doing everything yourself.

So head over to **www.InternetIncomeIntensive.com**
and take all my templates for free so that you can focus
on the finer things in life, while someone else does the
work for you.

174

- PART 3 -

THE BEGINNING

Why is the beginning at the
end? Well, read on and
find out...

Discovering blessings in dark times and deciding what to do about them.

AWESOME CONCLUDING
- CHAPTER -

COMING FULL CIRCLE

Discovering blessings in dark times and deciding what to do about them

Just as my Silent Sales Machine is a circle of endless possibilities, so is my story.

Looking back, all my dark times became blessings in disguise.

Had I not been a (compulsive) gambler, I wouldn't have lost all my tuition money in the UK.

And had I not lost all my tuition money in the UK, I wouldn't have discovered World of Warcraft as a cheap form of super addictive entertainment.

And had I not discovered World of Warcraft as a cheap form of super addictive entertainment, I wouldn't have nearly flunked out of university.

And had I not nearly flunked out of university, I wouldn't have been stuck at a dead-end job with a massive student loan to pay off.

And had I not been stuck at a dead-end job with a massive student loan to pay off, I wouldn't have tried to make money online.

And had I not tried to make money online, I wouldn't be where I am, or who I am, today.

The irony is that my addiction to WoW, which resulted in that dead-end job and massive student loan, was my saving grace. And it was only because of that addiction that I knew the game so thoroughly I could write guides on it. And make money off it.

So what I'm trying to say is everything happens for a reason. It's all connected.

Now, although I don't know you personally, and have no idea which season you may currently be in, just keep in mind that if you're stuck in your winter, this is what will later empower you.

Back when I was in my shower, getting wet but not showering, was the lowest point of my life.

That was when I was stuck in a rut and I simply could not see any way out. And yet, in retrospect, it was that very moment that I found strength. And it was only by going through it that I came out a better, wiser person.

179

Because I believe that times of adversity shape who we are.

It's up to us to decide whether we will allow adversity to make us bitter and hateful and remain trapped in that position forever. Or whether we will work to overcome it, and rise above it, and become better people because of it.

Everyone dies. Not everyone truly lives.

You've read my story.

You have your own. And I know it's powerful, but only if you take charge of it, and use it to your advantage.

Looking back at all the shit I went through, if I could go back and change anything, I wouldn't touch a thing.

In an alternate universe, if I had continued to study hard in university and retained my straight 'A's, I would have returned to Malaysia and easily been snapped up by a multinational corporation.

I wouldn't have to pay back a single cent from my conditional scholarship. Within a few short years I would be receiving a steady five-figure salary. I'd be on the fast track to corporate stability.

There would be no pressing need to Google 'How to make money online', and an even smaller desire to bother writing guides and selling them for a measly $7.

I would be comfortable. Maybe even wealthy. But would I be happy? Or have both the financial and time freedom that I so enjoy now? Probably not.

So what?

My life, and your life, is happening. Right now.

Don't look back and think, "What if?" or worse, "If only..."

I grew up on a physical farm, hated it, and ended up earning millions online through a digital farm.

It's funny. And strange. And ironic.

Look into yourself and know, for sure, what it is you really want out of your life. Because if you're currently living one that doesn't feel like your own, that doesn't bring you joy and happiness on a daily basis, then it's time to start a new chapter.

181

Take control and write your own story by making a change. Take a leap of faith and get uncomfortable.

Because though this book has come to an end, my story continues to be written by the decisions and actions I choose to make. Open up to the possibility and infinite potential that lies within you. And decide how you want your story to begin.

I believe that my work here is done. Yours has just begun.

THE BEGINNING

Claim Your FREE
Step-By-Step Online Training

My intention when I first set out to write this book was not only to tell my story, but to also share my knowledge. At this point I am hopeful for two outcomes. The first is that my words which summarized my life made you smile a little. And the second is that you got a good insight on the infinite possibilities of the Internet.

You've made it this far and if you've signed up for the free lifetime membership of **www.InternetIncomeIntensive.com** then you should have an even deeper understanding of making money online.

Yet, there's only so much information I could provide given the limitations of this physical book. If I've opened your eyes a little to the potential you have then I have accomplished my goal in creating this.

However, I must admit that everything I have given you is only a fraction of what is really out there. There are only so many things I can show you in text. Even in the videos I've provided online, nothing compares to having me bring you through the processes step-by-step in person.

It's because of this very reason that I have created a new video training for you that shows you how to do this.

As you may have noticed, I'm no different from anyone else. I'm nothing special.

I'm just a guy who was in a bad place, working a crappy dead-end job with a massive student loan hanging over his head.

But I got out.

Without any knowledge in programming, coding, graphic design and copywriting, I managed to generate multiple passive streams of income through the Internet.

And if I can do it, I *know* that you can too.

So if you are interested in taking your interest in making money online to a whole new level, then please join at that website.

I assure you that there's nothing like me training you over video. Not because I'm so damn good looking, but because I can guide you and show you HOW to get things done.

Head over to the **www.InternetIncomeIntensive.com** website and claim your FREE gifts now.

Scan this QR code for
FREE training videos on how to build a
personal brand online.

www.InternetIncomeIntensive.com

GRATITUDE

I've always had problems expressing how I truly feel and this section was one of the hardest to put into writing.

I would like to thank my parents. Mum, Dad, I know I gave you much grief and perhaps even disappointment while growing up. I do hope I've made you proud. I love you more than words can express and truly appreciate everything you have done for me.

To my brother, Peng Li, thank you for constantly looking out for me. You have continued to support me both professionally and personally throughout the years. You are a gem.

The three of you are a reminder to me to how truly blessed I am and how I literally struck the genetic lottery.

Shu Yiing, who has been through this entire ride of ups and downs, putting up with my crazy/eccentric/bipolar ways and sticking with me regardless of the outcome.

As for my colleagues over at Smobble, thank you for your daily inspiration and laughter throughout this journey. You guys are a daily dose of why life is awesome.

I owe particular gratitude to my writer and editor, Laila Zain. From managing the project to handling all my never-ending changes, quite simply the book wouldn't exist without you.

Sabri Ibrahim, thank you for your mad skills in designing and giving the images in this book life.

To my mentor, Joel Bauer, who has guided and inspired me throughout this process. I am forever a fan and indebted.

Success Resources, Richard Tan and Veronica Chew, who have been organizing my seminars and events that has allowed me to share my message and inspire participants from over 20+ countries worldwide through my workshops. You guys are family to me.

There were times I got tired and tried to take the easy way out. That strategy wasn't an option here thanks to Gerry Robert, President of Black Card Books, the company that published this book. Gerry worked diligently and helped keep my perfectionist mindset in check. Otherwise, we would still be on Chapter 2 right now.

189

Finally, I offer my appreciation and gratitude to you, the reader. I hope you enjoyed reading my story as much as I have had telling it. Feel free to let me know about your pursuit of freedom by writing to **pengjoon.com** or saying hi on Facebook (@pengjoon).

Website:

www.InternetIncomeIntensive.com

www.pengjoon.com

Facebook:

www.facebook.com/pengjoon

Twitter:

twitter.com/pengjoon

Instagram:

www.instagram.com/pengjoon